PROFESSIONAL ORCHESTRATION:

A PRACTICAL HANDBOOK -
Workbook

BY JOSEPH WAGNER
REVISED BY PETER LAWRENCE ALEXANDER

Professional Orchestration:
A Practical Handbook – Workbook
Copyright ©2009 by Peter Lawrence Alexander

Alexander Publishing
P.O. Box 1720
Petersburg, VA 23805
www.alexanderpublishing.com

Alexander Publishing is the
Publishing division of Alexander University, Inc.

Professional Orchestration is a service mark of Alexander University, Inc.

Paperback edition published 2009
ISBN-13: 978-0-939067-99-2

Printed in the United States of America

Cover design and layout by Caroline J. Alexander

Alexander, Peter Lawrence, 1950-

Table of Contents

Professional Orchestration:
A Practical Handbook - Workbook

With homework examples to be used for all three handbooks, From Piano to Strings, From Piano to Woodwinds, and From Piano to Orchestra.

This workbook is organized by the *Reference Chart of Keyboard Idioms*. Each section matches the same chapter number in all three handbooks, *From Piano to Strings, From Piano to Woodwinds, From Piano to Orchestra*. There's a bonus section called *Music Without Classification* which includes challenging works by Bach, Debussy, and Beethoven.

Turn to the next page for the *Reference Chart of Keyboard Idioms*

I. Broken Intervals

    1. Broken octaves
    2. Broken octaves with embellishments
    3. Broken octaves combined with thirds
    4. Broken sixths
    5. Broken thirds
    6. Broken sixths and thirds combined

II. Broken Chords

    1. Left-hand broken chords in close position
    2. Left-hand broken chords in open position
    3. Broken chords spaced for two hands
    4. Broken chords in right-hand with implied melodic line
    5. Broken chords with blocked melodic and rhythmic patterns
    6. Arpeggiated chords

III. Melodic Lines & Figurations

    1. Large melodic skips
    2. Outlining a melodic line
    3. Dividing a melodic line
    4. Melodic lines combined with repeated note patterns; nonmetrical passages
    5. Melodic settings: contrasts, comparative strengths, and repeated phrases

IV. Implied Bass Parts

V. Single-Note, Interval & Chord Repetitions

VI. Two- & Three-Part Music

    1. Homophonic
    2. Polyphonic
    3. Style mixtures

VII. Spacing Problems in the Middle Register

    1. Large harmonic gaps
    2. Sustained notes, intervals, and chords

VIII. Contrast Problems Conditioned by Dynamics

IX. Voice Leading

X. Obbligato or Added Secondary Parts Arranged from Harmonic Progressions

XI. Antiphonal Effects

XII. Tremolo Types

XIII. Dance Forms (Afterbeats)

How to Approach Each Example

All of the piano examples in the *Workbook* have been recorded in a separate package available for purchase from www.alexanderpublishing.com. Start by listening to each example numerous times to fix the music in your ear. Before scoring, double check the time signature and the tempo. For strings, before selecting your bowings, double check to see the tempo ranges at which each bowing is capable of being performed by a professional. For woodwinds, double check tempos for single, double and triple tongueings.

MIDI Mockups – First, check to insure that the articulations you select can perform at the designated tempos. This is especially true where repeated notes are written in the music. If you're doing the mockup just to check out your work, you can let the tempo slide. But if you're doing it to demonstrate a composition, especially a film score, the samples selected must be as accurate as possible.

> *Note:*
>
> *Professional Orchestration Volume 1: Solo Instruments and Instrumentation Notes* contains timings for bowings and woodwind/brass articulations.

Check the Harmony

It's always advisable to do an harmonic analysis to study the melody and the harmonization. In looking at the harmony, count the number of pitches in each vertical structure. For example, a vertical harmony may go from five pitches to seven pitches. In such cases, how will you assign the parts to strings or woodwinds? What if you need to add pitches? Which tones in the chord will you double? All of these are decisions that the composer/ orchestrator needs to make whether it's your composition or someone else's your scoring.

Check for Combinations

Each *Handbook* is complemented by a specific volume in the *Professional Orchestration* Series that covers combinations for each orchestral section. Within each *Handbook*, you'll find a chart of unisons for that instrumental section. These unique range charts enable you to spot color combinations that push the exercises to new levels in terms of giving you lots of choice for multiple solutions along with coloristic orchestration.

Handbook	Matching Text
From Piano to Strings	**Professional Orchestration Volume 2A:** *Orchestrating the Melody Within the String Section*
From Piano to Woodwinds	**Professional Orchestration Volume 2B:** *Orchestrating the Melody Within the Woodwinds and Brass*
From Piano to Orchestra	**Professional Orchestration Volume 3:** *Orchestrating the Melody by Combining Orchestral Sections*

Do Multiple Solutions

Having the unison range charts and the complementing *Professional Orchestration* titles gives you a significant advantage in that you can check your options to see how others have scored works in a similar range.

Study the following example, Chabrier's *Bourree Fantasque* then examine the options for string scoring I created—as shown on page viii.

Bourree Fantasque

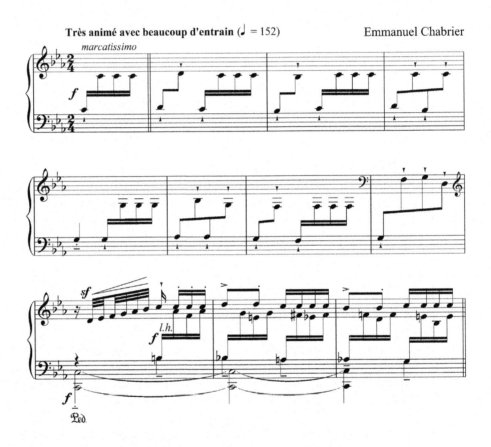

Très animé avec beaucoup d'entrain (♩ = 152)

Emmanuel Chabrier

Approaching the Unison Line

Look at the unison line by register by string instruments.
The first seven and a half bars the line is in the:

- low register of the violins then moving off the instrument at bar 6
- medium register of the violas staying completely in its range
- medium register of the cellos staying completely in its range.

Bowings and Tempos

The tempo is quarter note = 152 beats per minute. The French instructions say *tres anime avec beaucoup d'entrain*. Since I don't speak French I need to translate. You can find free translation on the web or use the translation feature available on Dashboard on the Mac. The translation is, "Very animated with much spirit." A Sousa march is at 120 BPM. So this tempo is about 30% faster.

In *Professional Orchestration Volume 1: Solo Instruments and Instrumentation Notes*, we worked out the tempos at which various bowings can be performed. Starting at bar 8 in the violins, there are four possible bowings that might work:

- **detache moyen**
- **sautille** — rapid spiccato without lifting the bow off the string (crisp, popcorn popping sound)
- **spiccato**
- **martele**

How do you know the bowing you want? The first place to start is by listening to the recorded piano example to gain an interpretation insight that might be transferable to the strings.

After listening to or playing the piano part, you draw on your musical experience to determine the most effective bow stroke that supports the composer's intent. To repeat, if you haven't built up that accumulated experience yet, do what most wise composers do — ask the advice of the person playing it, the violinist. Even Ravel did that! In fact, Ravel brought in a concert violinist to mark the bowings on the score before the parts were copied and put on the stands.

However, we're now in the Twenty First Century and there's YouTube. So if there's no violinist around, or you feel ultra embarrassed to ask, go to www.youtube.com and type in the bowing you're thinking about.

While no one wants to say this aloud, many string players consider composers and arrangers to be idiots when it comes to string bowings and will ignore what you wrote and redo it anyway. Even so! Bowings are part of your device and orchestral effects list. A bowing creates a certain sound, and to the best of your ability you need to mark your parts as best as possible.

Approaching the Five-Part Harmony

Bourree Fantasque

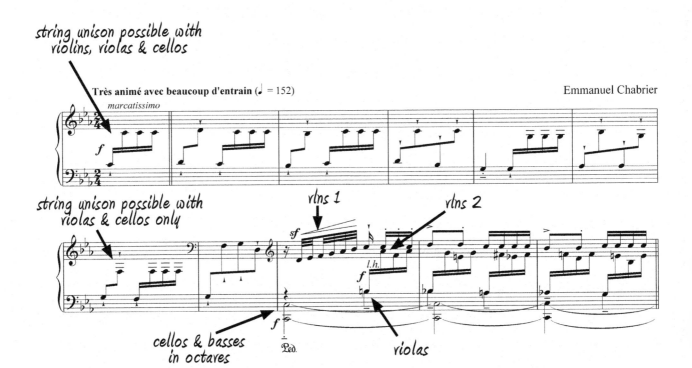

The graphic above shows what happens at bar 8 when the piece goes to five-part harmony. Look carefully for practical counterpoint applications 4 against 1 and 2 against 1. Once we get to this point, assigning the "notes" is pretty simple. But there are other decisions.

First Violins

The Violins 1 entrance is a D phrygian scale. Options are:

- Sul D (depends on the skill of the players being written for)
- Starting on the open D-string (with an open pitch) and crossing to the A-string
- Playing under a single bow
- Detache

Second Violins

I think the Second Violins are the make it or break it part of this example. 152BPM is blazingly fast for sixteenth notes. Notice that the first pitch of the sixteenth group is assigned down an octave. If you score this exactly, the Second Violins have a sixteenth rest which, at this tempo, requires considerable precision. I think that's a prescription for a performance problem, especially if performed by an amateur orchestra or students. So my inclination is to raise that first pitch on the sixteenth group up an octave so the Second Violins have a steady sixteenth note line to play.

Violas

There's a line over the notehead signifying that the quarter note part is to be performed for the full duration of the quarter note. The violas are performing a descending chromatic line. You could separate each pitch or play them all under a single bow.

Cellos and Basses

The cellos and basses are sustained playing in octaves. Another option is putting the violas on their lowest C (doubling the basses), and having the cellos perform the descending chromatic line. Or, you can double the violas and cellos on the C, and have the basses perform the descending line. This puts the basses in the range of the professional. Check the Alexander Publishing *String Positions Booklet* for details.

Options

Bars 8 to the end pretty much write themselves for assigning notes. The pick-ups going into bar 1 offer these possibilities:

- Violins 1 only up to bar 6 followed by Violas only, or Cellos only
- Violins 2 only up to bar 6 followed by Violas only, or Cellos only
- Violins 1 + 2 up to bar 6 followed by Violas + Cellos
- Violas only up to bar 8
- Cellos only up to bar 8
- Violas + Cellos only up to bar 8
- Violins 1 + Violins 2 + Violas + Cellos up to bar 6 then Violas + Cellos only
- Violins 1 + Violas + Cellos up to bar 6 then Violas + Cellos only
- Violins 2 + Violas + Cellos up to bar 6 then Violas + Cellos only

So far I've worked out eleven different possibilities for just 8 bars. Are there others?

Please turn to the next page for an example of one solution I created:

Bourree Fantasque - Orchestrated for String Ensemble

Emmanuel Chabrier
orchestrated by Peter L. Alexander

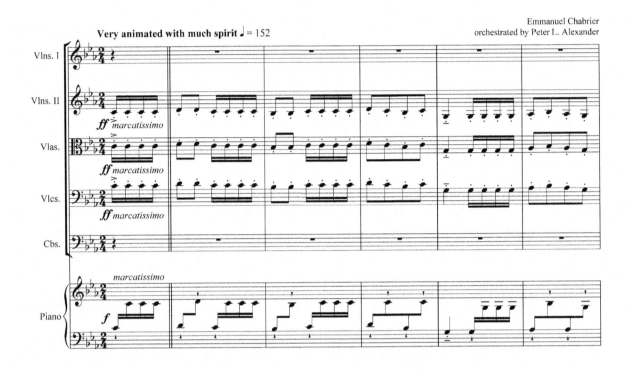

Homework Applications

By taking this approach for each example, you'll develop a wealth of solutions. By recording your answers with a good orchestral sample library, you'll discover ahead of time what will probably work, and not work. You'll also be developing your MIDI editing, recording and mixing skills, which is a great side bonus!

And now, on to the examples.

Chapter 1

Broken Intervals

The term "broken intervals," as used here, refers to their movement in sequence as distinguished from intervals occurring in broken-chord formations. Broken intervals, in this category, usually have a dual purpose: (1) they maintain rhythmic patterns idiomatically, and (2) they complete harmonic progressions. Literal scoring for orchestral instruments is possible only at slow tempos. The following examples are to be arranged as shown in the *Handbooks* under this heading.

1. Broken Octaves

Étude

Presto con energia

Sergei Prokofiev, Op. 2, No. 4

2. Broken Octaves With Embellishments

Finale from Sonata No. 7

Joseph Haydn

3. Broken Octaves Combined With Thirds

This excerpt includes several entries in this classification. The extremes of dynamic range permit a corresponding variety of range extensions and sonorities.

Please see next page for example.

The Horseman

4. Broken Sixths

Waltz

5. Broken Thirds

Reduce these thirds to four-part harmony outlining and sustaining the melody and bass parts. Retain the sixteenth-note rhythm in the two middle parts. The complete excerpt should be phrased *legato*.

Saint Nicolas

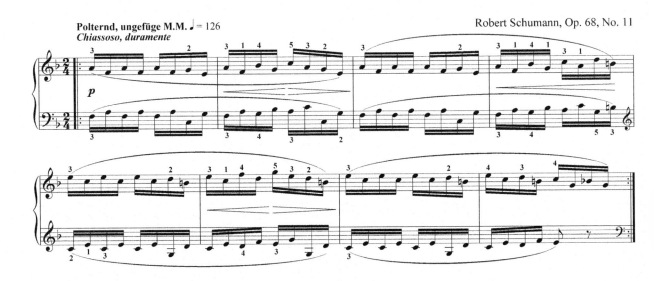

6. Broken Sixths and Thirds Combined

Intermezzo

Broken Chords

1. Left-Hand Broken Chords in Close Position

First Arabesque

In *Pièce Héroïque* for organ, the melody should be written in octaves with an inside filler. The pedal point in the bass part can also be extended an octave higher.

Pièce Héroïque

Allegro Maestoso

César Franck

2. Left-Hand Broken Chords in Open Position

Fantasie Impromptu

Frederic Chopin, Op. 66

Serenata Andaluza

Manuel de Falla

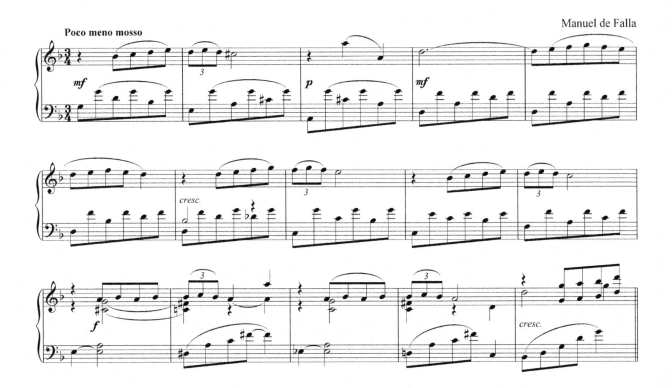

3. Broken Chords Spaced for Two Hands

Chords in this category should first be reduced to four-part writing with the highest and lowest notes sustained as melody and bass parts. In the *Rondo* on the facing page, these parts would be in half notes. The rhythmic figuration should be maintained in the two inside parts. (See the examples in the *Handbooks* under this heading.) This would be a good example to experiment with, adding one or two *obbligatos* (in the high treble and tenor ranges), as explained in each *Handbook*.

Rondo

Moderato e grazioso

Ludwig van Beethoven, Op. 51, No. 1

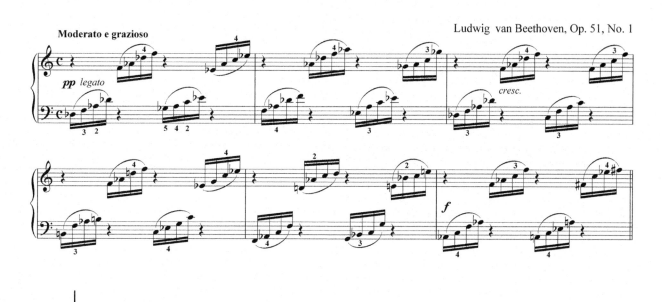

Arietta

Poco andante e sostenuto

Edvard Grieg, Op. 12, No. 1

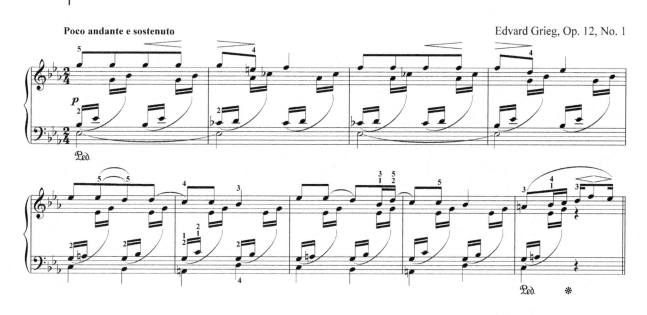

4. Broken Chords in Right-Hand With Implied Melodic Line

In scoring the next two examples, keep the implied melodic lines free of the inside harmony parts. The bass parts should also be detached from the two inside rhythmic harmony parts. Vary the orchestration on the thematic repetitions.

Air

George Frederic Handel

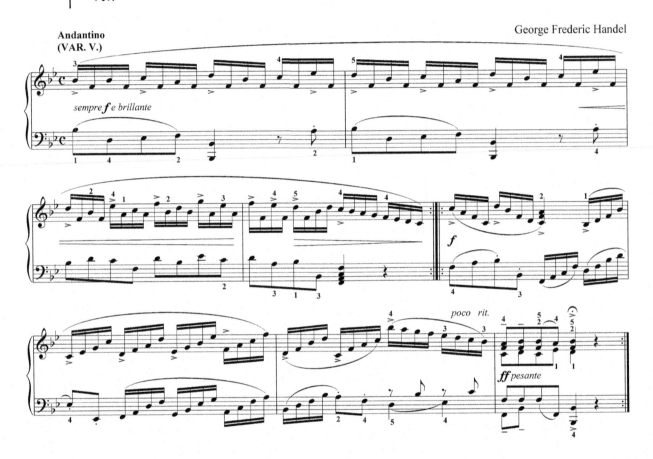

Impromptu

Allegretto (♩ = 132)
(TRIO)

Franz Schubert, Op. 142, No. 2

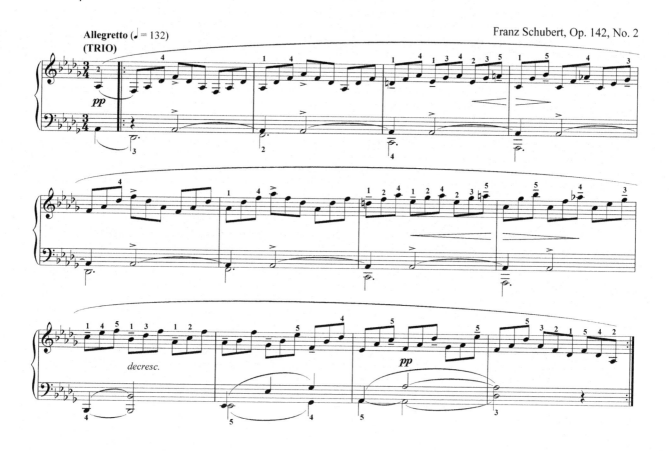

5. Broken Chords With Blocked Melodic and Rhythmic Patterns

Passacaille

George Frederic Handel

Allegro con brio

6. Arpeggiated Chords

The two following excerpts are most desirable for full orchestra. The *arpeggios* in both can be scored as follows: (1) Arrange them idiomatically for appropriate strings. (2) Arrange them as broken chords for strings or woodwinds and give the full *arpeggios* to the harp. In the Mendelssohn excerpt, supply the harmony for the first measure and continue it in accordance with the rhythmic pattern given by the composer. The Rachmaninov excerpt requires sustained middle harmony parts as indicated in the third measure.

Rondo Capriccioso

Felix Mendelssohn, Op. 14

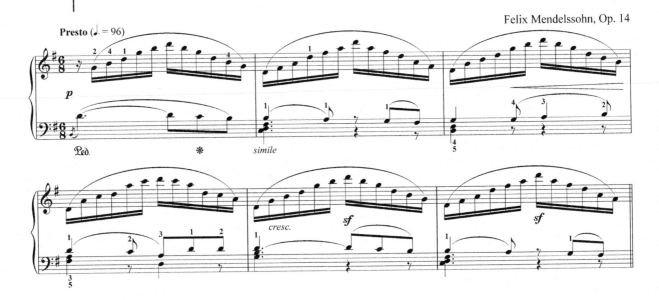

Prelude in G Minor

Alla marica (♩=108)
Un poco meno mosso

Sergei Rachmaninov, Op. 23, No. 5

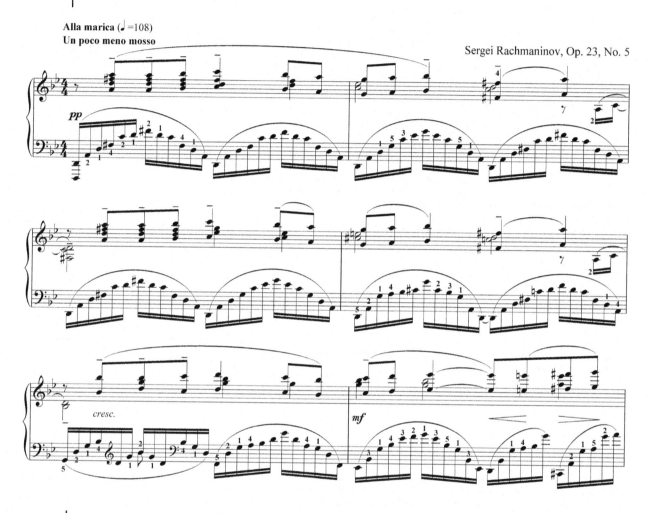

Chapter 3

Melodic Lines & Figurations

1. Large Melodic Skips

At fast tempos it is advisable to rearrange themes of this kind for two voices, yet always retaining both the rhythmic patterns and interval changes.

Please see next page for example.

Carnival Scene

Edvard Grieg, Op. 19, No. 3

2. Outlining a Melodic Line

Two plans of outlining are suggested here: (1) above the melody, and (2) sustained an octave lower, combined with the lowest theme note on each beat.

Second Arabesque

Allegretto scherzando

Claude Debussy

3. Dividing a Melodic Line

Divide the entire treble part for two or more voices as required. Parts in the bass range will also need considerable revision to provide consistent voice textures.

Please see next page for example.

Characteristic Piece No. 2

Allegro vivace (♩. = 72)

Felix Mendelssohn, Op. 7, No. 2

4. Melodic Lines Combined With Repeated Note Patterns

In scoring this excerpt, retain the *tessitura* of the repeated notes but rearrange the chord positions starting in measure twenty-one.

Sonata No. 27

Sonata No. 12 - Rondo

Wolfgang Amadeus Mozart

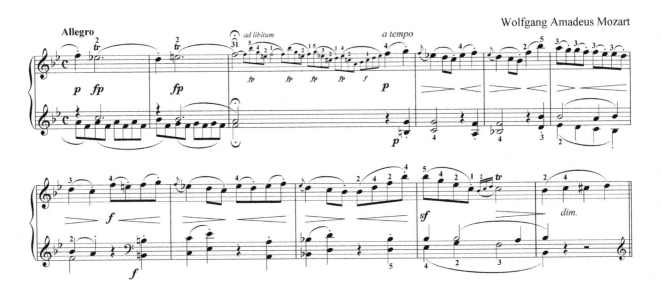

5. Melodic Settings: Contrasts, Comparative Strengths and Repeated Phrases

These four-measure excerpts, taken from eight-measure phrases, illustrate one composer's approach to seeking contrast with the same thematic material at different dynamic levels. The orchestration of these phrases should explore the full potentialities of each section, reserving the full orchestra for the two *fortissimo* passages. **Note:** Observe the *obbligato* in the second brace [b]. It could be varied and repositioned for the other variations.

A Joyous Party

[a]

Ernst Dohnányi, Op. 13, No. 8

[b]

Chapter 4

Implied Bass Parts

A number of the previous examples required the extracting of implied bass parts from chord formations. The following excerpt presents music which calls for sustained tenor and bass parts combined with a pedal point. By starting the implied bass part on the second beat of the third measure and treating it as a suspension, the effect intended by the composer can be realized. This plan changes in measure eleven.

Please see next page for example.

Finale from Sonatina

Bela Bartók

Single-Note, Interval & Chord Repetitions

The examples for this category have been selected so that they can be represented in their most familiar forms. Each excerpt should be rearranged idiomatically for orchestral instruments, as illustrated in the *Handbooks* under this heading.

1. Repeated Notes — Without Rests

Bear Dance No. X - (Ten Easy Pieces for Piano)

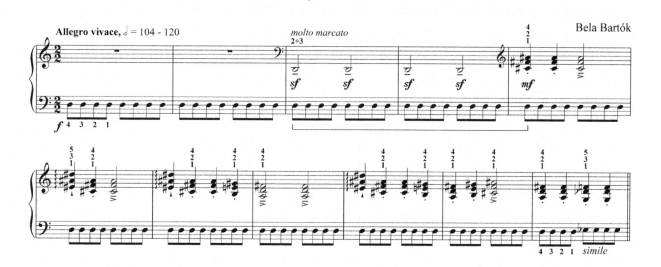

2. Repeated Notes — With Rests

Novelette

Robert Schumann, Op. 21, No. 4

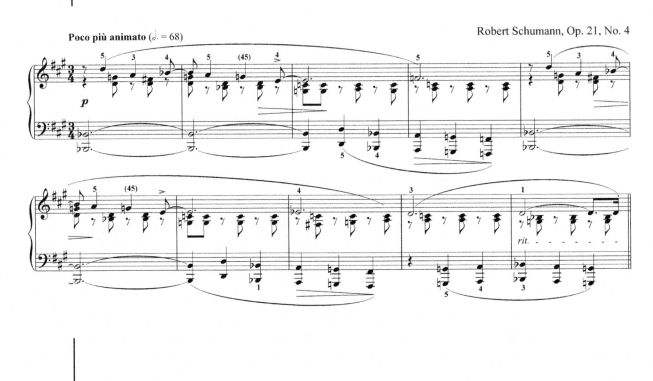

Rondo

Ludwig van Beethoven, Op. 51, No. 1

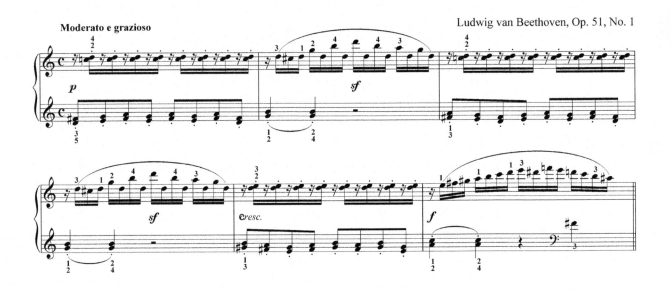

3. Repeated Intervals as Afterbeats

Valses Nobles (No. 6)

Franz Schubert, Op. 77

4. Repeated Chords

Suggestion Diabolique

Sergei Prokofiev, Op. 4, No. 4

5. Repeated Notes, Intervals, and Chords Spaced for Alternating Hands

Bourrée Fantasque

Très animé avec beaucoup d'entrain (♩ = 152)

Emmanuel Chabrier

Le Polichinelle

Heitor Villa-Lobos

Ballade

Chapter 6

Two- & Three-Part Music

Most of the music included up to this point has been homophonic. The voice textures have often been inconsistent, thereby requiring considerable revision, as will be the case with similar music to follow. The next excerpts illustrate three varieties of homophonic styles and textures.

Please see next page for example.

1. Homophonic

Rigaudon

Andante

Oriental - (from Danzas Españolas)

Enrique Granados, Op. 5, No. 2

2. Polyphonic

Polyphonic music in its most strict forms (canon and fugue, without doublings, fillers, or harmonization), is comparatively rare in orchestral music. In fugal scoring, some doubling in octaves is permissible, notably in bass parts and for principal thematic material emphasis. Occasional outlining and sustaining may also be necessary and even desirable. The harmonized canon by Schumann on page 35 needs clarity for the two thematic lines in contrast to and with the harmony parts whenever possible. Review this category in the *Handbooks*.

Please see next page for examples.

Fugue No. 21 - (from the Well-tempered Clavichord)

A Canon

Nicht schnell und mit innigem Ausdruck M.M. ♩ = 72
(Moderato e con intima espressione)

Robert Schumann, Op. 68, No. 27

3. Style Mixtures

Style mixtures (juxtapositions of homophonic and polyphonic passages) provide a great source of organic strength, continuity, and contrast for symphonic music. Scoring in this style should be along the lines discussed under this heading in the *Handbooks*.

Allegretto in C Minor

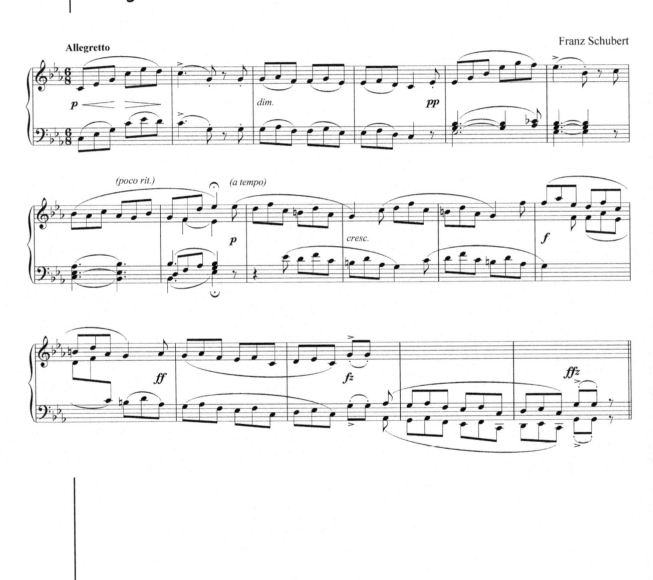

Franz Schubert

Warum?

Robert Schumann, Op. 12, No. 3

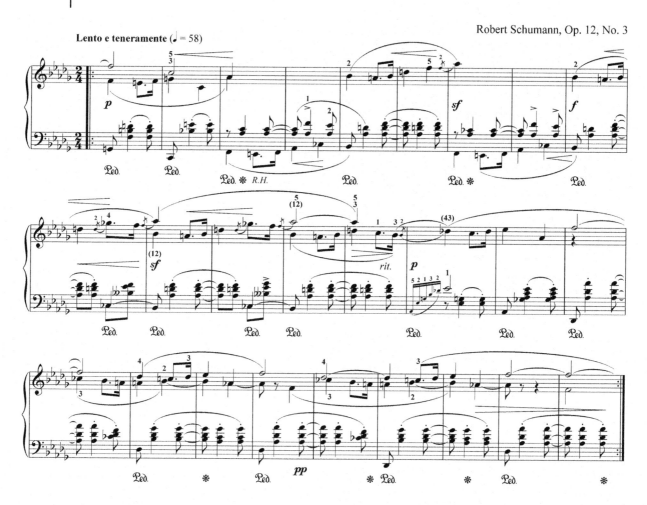

Träumerei

Richard Strauss, Op. 9, No. 4

Chapter 7

Spacing Problems
in the Middle Register

Both entries under this classification have been presented as secondary considerations in many of the previous categories. They should now be reexamined as isolated, major problems concerned with orchestral balance and sonority.

1. Large Harmonic Gaps

In the example on the following page, fillers in the middle register are needed for the first two and one-half measures of each four-measure phrase.

Please see next page for example.

Sevilla

2. Sustained Notes, Intervals and Chords

Sustained parts, indispensable for full orchestra starting in the third measure, can be extracted from the upper notes of the broken chords and the implied bass notes.

Rhapsody

Johannes Brahms, Op. 79, No. 2

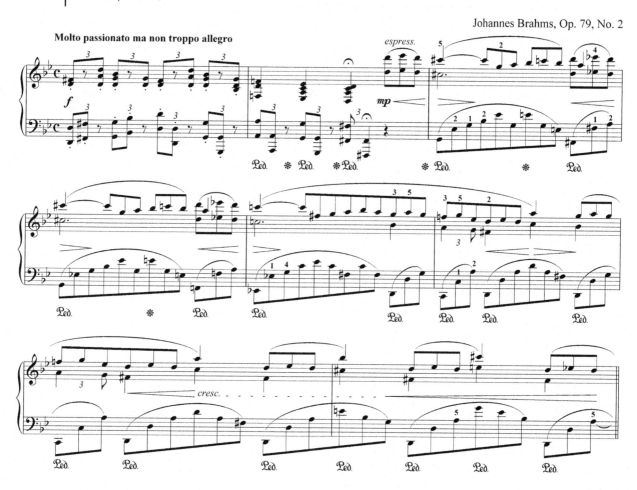

Contrast Problems Conditioned by Dynamics

Consult the *Handbooks* under this heading for suggested ways of scoring similar or identical phrases with different dynamics. Example [a] below is scored *piano*, while [b] is *fortissimo*.

Impromptu

[a] Allegro (♩. = 69)

Franz Schubert, Op. 90, No. 2

[b] *ben marcato*

Sonatina No. 1

Chapter 9

Voice Leading

The place and problem of good voice leading is strikingly apparent in the Chopin excerpt on the next page. In scoring it, rearrange the voice structure of the harmony and bass so that they can be maintained consistently. Grace notes that are melodic embellishments should be retained whenever practicable. Those that are distinctly chordal, as in measures 7 and 8, can generally be eliminated altogether or incorporated as part of the harmonic texture. Review this category in the *Handbooks*.

Please see next page for example.

Nocturne in G Minor

Frederic Chopin, Op. 37, No. 1

Chapter 10

Obbligato or Added Secondary Parts Arranged from Harmonic Progressions

A dd an *obbligato* part in the tenor register and a second, more rapid counterpoint above the melody. Plan both parts so that their greatest momentum and intensity starts in the twelfth measure. Consult this category in the *Handbooks* for directions and illustrations. The final "8 va." can be omitted; the others are optional. Work for maximum sonority and brilliance starting at the 2/4 measure.

Please see next page for example.

Gibralter - (from Album de Viajo)

Joaquin Turina

Chapter 11

Antiphonal Effects

Alternate the string and woodwind sections as given in the *Handbooks* under this heading. The sextolet (a double triplet, or a group of six equal notes played in the time of four) may be scored either in octaves or as broken chords. Seek maximum brilliance within the instrumentation of the Classic orchestra.

Please see next page for example.

Serious Variations

Felix Mendelssohn, Op. 54

Chapter 12

Tremolo Types

Form octaves for the highest treble notes of this Mozart excerpt starting in measure five and score this passage as a measured tremolo. The arpeggiated chords in *Rhapsody No. 2* on pages 52-53 are to be scored as unmeasured, fingered tremolos.

Sonata No. 9

Wolfgang Amadeus Mozart

Serious Variations (No. 17)

Felix Mendelssohn, Op. 54

Rhapsody No. 2

Ernst Dohnányi

Rhapsody No. 2 (continued)

(Lo stesso tempo)   Ibid.

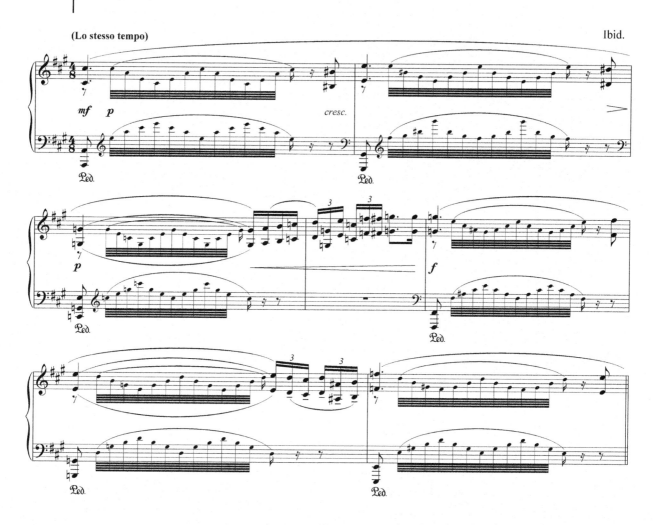

Chapter 13

Dance Forms

These dance excerpts have been selected primarily to provide music having characteristic afterbeats. In scoring them give consideration to other pertinent entries in the *Reference Chart*.

Please see next page for example.

Mazurka in B Flat Major

Frederic Chopin, Op. 7, No. 1

Polonaise (Military)

Allegro con brio

Frederic Chopin, Op. 40, No. 1

Waltz No. 3

Italian Polka

Allegretto (*not fast*)

Sergei Rachmaninov

Chapter 14

Music Without Classification

(Recommended for Special Assignments)

Fugue No. 5 in D Major
(from the Well-tempered Clavichord)

Johann Sebastian Bach

Fugue No. 5 in D Major (continued)

Nocturne in D Flat

Claude Debussy

Sonata in C Minor

First Movement—Exposition

Allegro molto e con brio M.M. ♩. = 69

Ludwig van Beethoven, Op. 10, No. 1

Psalm XXIX

Male Chorus & Two Pianos

Joseph Wagner

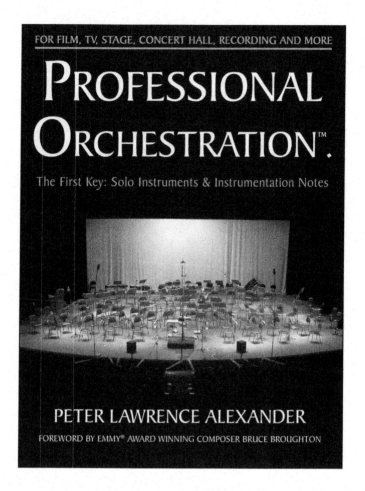

PROFESSIONAL ORCHESTRATION™. VOLUME I
THE FIRST KEY: SOLO INSTRUMENTS & INSTRUMENTATION NOTES
PETER LAWRENCE ALEXANDER

Recommended by winners of the Academy®, Grammy® and Emmy® Awards, *Professional Orchestration*™ is the first multi-volume series in orchestration from an American publisher that teaches the devices and orchestral combinations, which before now have been known by only a privileged few. It's also the only orchestration book whose instrumentation notes were checked and edited by members of the Hollywood studio musician elite. Features full page/full score examples on an 8.25 x 11 page. Optional *Professional Mentor*™ workbook and audio package from eClassical available for separate purchase.

"The best orchestration book since Forsyth"

- Jerry Goldsmith
Winner of both the Academy® & Emmy® Awards, USA

ISBN: 978-0-939067-70-1

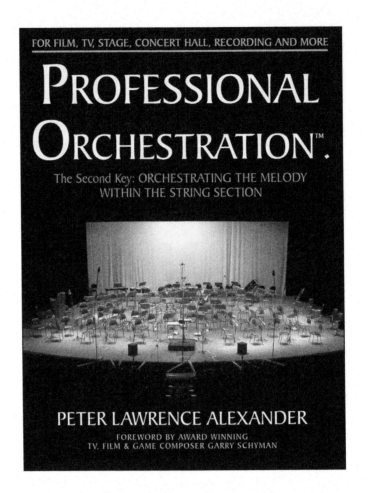

PROFESSIONAL ORCHESTRATION™. VOLUME 2A
THE SECOND KEY: ORCHESTRATING THE MELODY
WITHIN THE STRING SECTION
PETER LAWRENCE ALEXANDER

Imagine learning the scoring techniques creating the "Hollywood Sound" usually known by only a few top professional film orchestrators and composers. Now for the very first time, starting with *Professional Orchestration™, Volume 2A: Orchestrating the Melody Within the String Section*, the hidden doors on the techniques you've been hearing in the scores of John Williams, Jerry Goldsmith and others for years, are, at last, finally open. Thus, after months of painstaking research, the "secret formulas" are secret no more. Loaded with references from 35 works in a large full page/full score format (that you can MIDI mock-up at your leisure) are 63 techniques referenced meticulously in the low, medium, high and very high registers which are matched to the optional MP3 audio package (available separately) where excerpts are heard in the musical context of the scores.

"I would highly recommend this book to any student or working professional wishing to learn or expand their knowledge of orchestration. If you intend to work professionally the skills imparted by the studies presented here will be of enormous benefit and will give you a professional advantage for your entire career."
- Garry Schyman
Award winning game composer, Bio Shock, USA

ISBN: 978-0-939067-06-0

Available from www.alexanderpublishing.com or through your local book store.

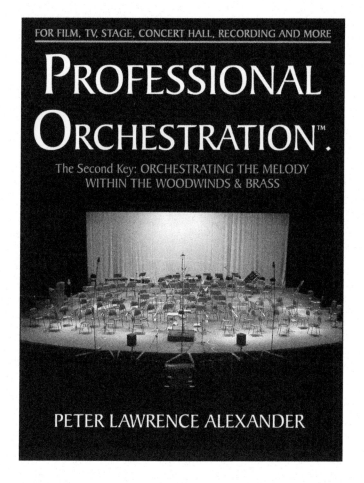

PROFESSIONAL ORCHESTRATION™. VOLUME 2B
THE SECOND KEY: ORCHESTRATING THE MELODY WITHIN THE WOODWINDS & BRASS
PETER LAWRENCE ALEXANDER

Professional Orchestration™, Volume 2B: Orchestrating the Melody Within the Woodwinds & Brass, completes the *Second Key of Professional Orchestration,* which covers orchestrating the melody in each orchestral section. With the full page/full score examples, this represents nearly 1,000 pages of orchestration instruction just for this single technique.

As with *Volume 2A,* each technique is organized by the low, medium, high and very high registers, which are matched to the optional MP3 audio package (available separately) where excerpts are heard in the musical context of the scores.

ISBN: 978-0-939067-93-0

Available from www.alexanderpublishing.com or through your local book store.

CPSIA information can be obtained
at www.ICGtesting.com
Printed in the USA
BVOW09s1915131116

467696BV00037B/161/P